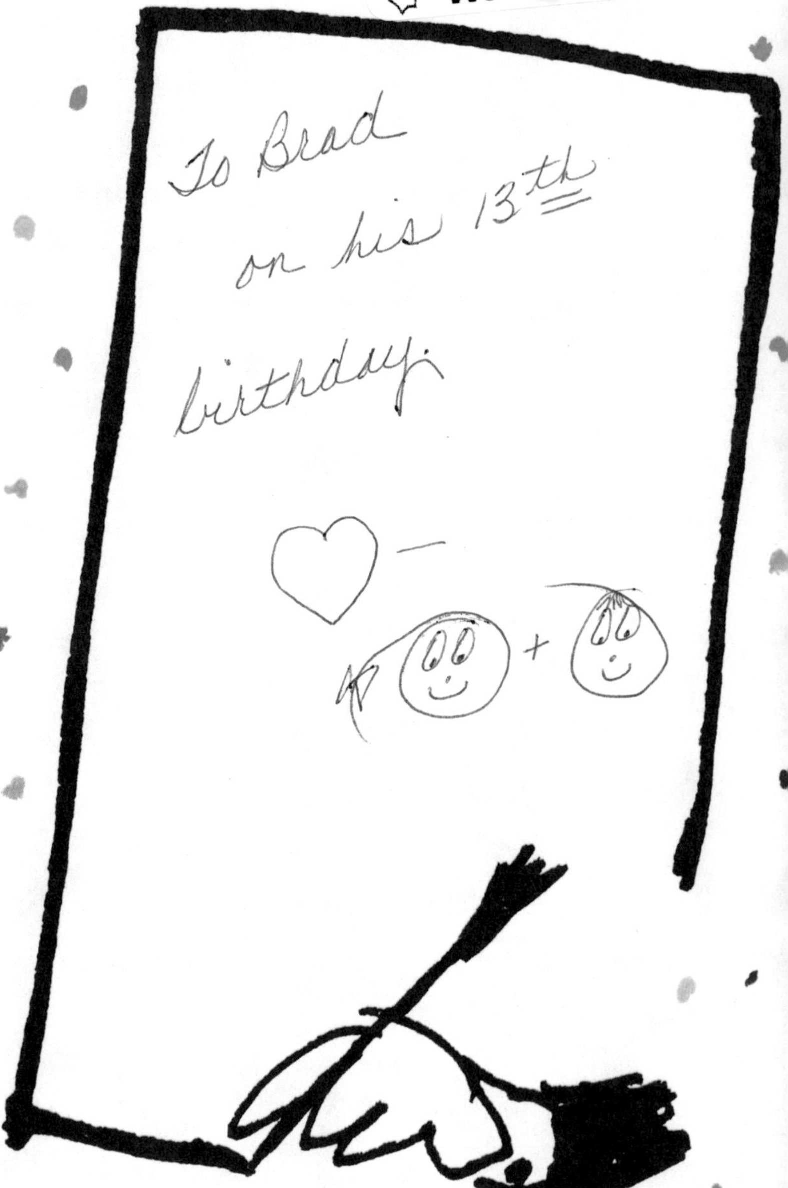
To Brad
on his 13th
birthday

MAY 22

Natalis Press, Inc.
New York, NY

Also Published by Natalis Press
Your Birthday
A book for each day of the year

The Happy Birthday Book

Copyright 1993 by Natalis Press, Inc.
New York, New York

Art Direction: James Victore
Designer: Cheryl Knippenburg

Contents

Much happiness is overlooked
because it doesn't cost anything.

Anonymous

What Happened on Your Birthday

May 22, 1983

Two Americans aged 50 and 51 reach 24,100 feet as they work their way toward the summit of 29,028-foot Mount Everest. They are attempting to become the oldest climbers to conquer the world's highest peak.

May 22, 1902

Crater Lake in Oregon is established as a National Park. At 1,932 feet, it is the deepest lake in the U.S. It was formed when a volcano in the Cascade Range in Oregon collapsed about 6,850 years ago, after which rain and snow gradually filled it.

May 22, 1957

Prince Aly Khan divorces "Love Goddess" actress Rita Hayworth for the second time.

May 22, 1976

Following a landmark court decision in a case instituted by her parents, Karen Ann Quinlan, who has been comatose since last year, is removed from life support systems.

May 22, 1843

Heeding the encouraging reports sent back by fur traders, early pioneers, and missionaries, some 1,000 men, women, and children set out for Oregon's Wilmette Valley from Independence, Missouri, carrying in their wagons everything they must use for a new life. They will follow the Oregon Trail, first used by fur trappers in the 1820s. The trail follows the Platte River past Fort Laramie in Wyoming, across the North Platte and the barren country beyond to the Sweetwater River. From there it crosses the Rocky Mountains at a wide gap known as South Pass. Beyond the Continental Divide, the trail forks, one way leading south, the other on to their goal, which they will reach in October. Within three years, 4,000 more settlers will follow, firmly establishing the entire Oregon Country northward to the 49th parallel as belonging to the United States.

May 22, 1972

Hungarian-born Laszlo Toth attacks Michelangelo's statue *Pieta* in St. Peter's Basilica in Rome. As he shatters the Virgin's arm with a hammer, the deranged assailant shouts that he is Jesus Christ.

May 22, 1924

The aviators of three Army planes on a 27,000-mile flight around the world that began in Seattle are greeted by cheering crowds in Tokyo. They successfully flew the 878 miles between the Aleutian island of Attu and the Kurile Islands in Japan with one stop on the Kamchatka Peninsula. They thus became the first to fly across the Pacific Ocean. The majority of Japanese aviators had considered it impossible.

May 22, 1959

President Eisenhower appoints Benjamin Davis to the rank of Air Force major general, the first African-American to achieve this rank in the U.S. armed forces.

May 22, 1912

The liner *Majestic* leaves London bound for New York. There are only 13 first class passengers. On the busy transatlantic schedule, the ship replaces the *Titanic*, which sank on April 15.

May 22, 1979

Dan White, former San Francisco city employee, is convicted of voluntary manslaughter for shooting and killing San Francisco's mayor, George Moscone, and city supervisor Harvey Milk. White's lawyers used what becomes known as the "Twinkie defense," claiming their client became deranged from overconsumption of junk food.

May 22, 1912

Norwegian Captain Roald Amundsen is greeted by enthusiastic crowds as he reaches Montevideo, Uruguay on his return from his discovery of the South Pole last December 14.

May 22, 1953

The presidential hideaway in Maryland is renamed Camp David in honor of President Eisenhower's father and grandson. It was formerly called Shangri-la.

May 22, 1967

New Orleans District Attorney James Garrison asserts that former C.I.A. employees and not Lee Harvey Oswald killed President John F. Kennedy.

May 22, 1927

Yesterday Captain Charles A. Lindbergh became the first person to fly the Atlantic Ocean solo. He landed at Le Bourget Field in Paris at 10:20 PM, 33 and one-half hours after his *Spirit of St. Louis* struggled into the air at Roosevelt Field in New York, 3,610 miles away. He says the reception he received by the wildly enthusiastic crowd was the most dangerous part of the trip. Amusingly, Lindbergh had not anticipated the French popular reponse: Fearing he would not be recognized in France, he carried with him a letter of introduction from Colonel Theodore Roosevelt.

May 22, 1953

President Eisenhower signs a bill giving coastal states off-shore oil rights within their historic boundaries.

May 22, 1908

At Hammondsport, New York, a man named J. Newell Williams flies a curious machine he calls a "Helicopter." It is built like a revolving fan, with long inclining planes propelled by a motor at the foot of a mast. Loaded with ballast equal to the weight of a man, the curious machine rises eighteen inches from the ground.

May 22, 1949

Nearly four years after the end of World War II, Russia announces it will return the last 95,000 Japanese prisoners of war, except those to be tried for war crimes.

May 22, 1932

Amelia Earhart Putnam arrives in London after flying from Ireland, where she landed yesterday, becoming the first woman to fly the Atlantic Ocean solo. At 13 hours, 30 minutes, her flight also sets a new record for crossing the Atlantic. It began the day before yesterday at Harbor Grace, Newfoundland, five years to the day after Charles Lindbergh lifted off from Roosevelt Field in New York. Because her plane's altimeter was broken, the daring aviatrix was forced to skim the waves during most of the flight, during which she battled a storm for some 500 miles. She also endured a very real risk of fire from flames leaping out of the craft's exhaust. Tonight she will sleep in the comfort of the United States Embassy.

May 22, 1948

President Truman urges Congress to make Alaska a state, citing its strategic importance.

May 22, 1926

The 520,000-acre Great Smoky Mountain National Park is authorized. The Smokies are within the Appalachian mountain system and extend some 50 miles, forming the boundary between Tennessee and North Carolina. They are among the oldest mountains on earth and the highest in the U.S. east of the Black Hills.

May 22, 1955

The General Assembly of the Presbyterian Church in the U.S.A. approves women as ministers.

May 22, 1908

The luxury liner *Lusitania* arrives off Sandy Hook Light House headed for New York. It embarked from Liverpool and will complete the voyage in 4 days, 20 hours, and 22 minutes. This is a new record for an Atlantic Ocean crossing. The great ship also set a new record for the longest day's run and the highest average speed, 24.83 knots.

May 22, 1900

A dispute between a railroad and a property owner comes to a bizarre ending in New Jersey. After he purchased the property, Mr. Smith discovered that a spur of the railroad's track projected onto it. When the railroad refused to move either the track or an old a box car parked on it, he sawed the car in half and removed the portion projecting onto his property.

May 22, 1922

One of the shortest revolutions on record ends in Nicaragua when dissidents are compelled by U.S. Marines to give up a government fort seized and held for only eight hours.

May 22, 1932

The nation watches as New York City's mayor Jimmy Walker is embattled in a major corruption scandal that may force his resignation. A financier and officer of a bus manufacturer is tracked down in London and forced to return to testify about a $10,000 payment to the colorful mayor.

May 22, 1949

The nation is shocked at the news of the suicide of James A. Forrestal. The former Secretary of Defense leaped from the window of his room at the Bethesda Naval Hospital, where he has been under treatment for nervous exhaustion.

May 22, 1903

Seven years ago, George W. Carmack and two Indian companions, "Skookum" Jim and "Tagish" Charlie, hit the mother lode on Bonanaza Creek, a tributary of the Klondike River. Their discovery launched a stampede of thousands of gold seekers to the Yukon. Gold continues to come out of the area in ever-increasing amounts. Banks at Dawson, the capital of the Yukon Territory, are buying more than $1,250,000 in dust every two days.

May 22, 1924

13-year-old Bobby Franks, son of a wealthy retired Chicago watchmaker, was kidnapped and senselessly murdered in a crime that has drawn national attention. The kidnappers demanded $10,000 ransom, which is now the amount of the reward posted for their capture.

To Celebrate
Your May Birthday

If it's 1714 and you live someplace civilized (Boston, Philadelphia and New York are your only choices), you might have an opportunity to view a 7-foot tall, 12-foot long, one-humped Arabian camel at the first recorded exhibit of exotic wildlife in America.

If it's 1816 lock the doors, pull down the window shades, and join the latest dance craze. The "risqué waltz" is condemned by ministers, teachers, and parents because it requires that men and women hold each other instead of just touching fingertips.

If it's 1860 one of the new "dime novels," featuring the adventures of Calamity Jane, Kit Carson, Dick Deadwood and the like, might be among your gifts.

If it's 1877 and you're a dog-lover, you can skip dinner in a fancy club or restaurant in favor of visiting the first official dog show in the U.S., held at the Hippodrome in New York City.

If it's 1889 take a birthday cruise to France to see the stunningly avant garde architecture of the Eiffel Tower in Paris, completed this month for the opening of the Universal Exhibition.

If it's 1893 get your date to take you up and down and round and round on the first Ferris Wheel. Installed at the World's Columbian Exposition in Chicago at a cost of $300,000, the big toy is 250 feet in diameter.

If it's 1896 by yourself a present—a new sewing machine or perhaps a party dress—with the first trading stamps, issued by the Sperry & Hutchinson Company of Jackson, Michigan.

If it's 1904 ask your date (or your parents) to take you to the St. Louis World's Fair. Instead of birthday cake, you can celebrate with one of the first ice cream cones, created by a Syrian pastry chef who spoons ice cream into thin waffles when he runs out of clean dishes.

If it's 1915   and you've been a very good kid, you might spend your birthday setting up your new electric train set. Model trains used to be a rich man's hobby, but the new bright enamel sets from American Flyer are priced for everyone at $10. Wives, take note: not only little boys are interested.

If it's 1916   you can spend your birthday lazily working out the first crossword puzzles, created by journalist Arthur Wynne for the Sunday supplement to *The New York Times*.

If it's 1918   you're probably hoping for a Raggedy Ann doll, just designed by cartoonist Johnny Gruelle.

If it's 1921   you and an art-loving companion can travel to Washington, D.C to visit the Philip's Gallery, America's first museum of modern art.

If it's 1931   take in the breathtaking view from the top of the Empire State Building, the world's tallest, dedicated this month. Beware of large apes wrestling with airplanes.

If it's 1931   you can play "Happy Birthday" and impress your neighbors at the same time with your new Steinway Piano ($875).

If it's 1933 you might be honored (or embarrassed) at your musical birthday greeting when you receive one of the first singing telegrams, debuting this year.

If it's 1935 the birthday present of choice is a new Mickey Mouse watch, yours for $3.

If it's 1935 and you've been a very good girl, you might receive a blonde, blue-eyed, curly-haired, oh-so-adorable Shirley Temple doll, selling for $3. Party dress and patent leather Mary Janes are extra.

If it's 1939 enjoy an elegant three-course meal at the New York Yacht Club, plus entertainment by Fats Waller, all for $1.50.

If it's 1940 be *au courant* and patriotic by having a dish of M & M chocolate candies alongside the cake and ice cream. Invented for the U.S military, the candy that "melts in your mouth, not in your hand" is designed to give GIs a treat without giving them sticky trigger fingers.

If it's 1948 go wild with up to "31-plus" flavors newly available when two small ice cream merchants combine forces to create the first Baskin-Robbins ice cream parlor.

If it's 1949 take instant photos of your birthday party with the new Polaroid Land Camera, going on sale for $89.75. The camera produces a finished photo in just 60 seconds.

If it's 1950 savor a thick, juicy birthday steak and put off paying the check when you join Diner's Club, the first credit card plan in the U.S.

If it's 1964 the preferred weird gift is a pudgy-faced, flared-nostriled, jug-eared, shock-haired troll doll: $5.95 for an adult troll, $1.95 for a baby.

If it's 1964 and you don't need a gourmet meal to make you happy, you can munch a McDonald's hamburger, 15 cents, for your birthday dinner.

If it's 1971 forget about the mortgage, the car payments, and the grocery bills and celebrate with a $5,000 bottle of Chateau Lafite Rothschild champagne.

If it's 1976 splurge. Be among the first to travel from London or Paris to Washington, D.C. in less than four hours via the supersonic Concorde jet. It begins regular flights this month.

If it's 1978 and you've got money to burn, you could celebrate your birthday at Resorts International Hotel Casino in Atlantic City, the first legalized U.S. gambling venue outside of Nevada, which opens this month.

If it's 1945 you can spend your birthday week on a New York State dude ranch for only $29.

If it's 1928 treat yourself to a feather boa, available at Best & Co. for $32.50.

Fellow Birthday Bigwigs

William Sturgeon May 22, 1783; Physicist; he developed the electromagnet and performed other important research related to electric current.

Gerard de Nerval May 22, 1808; French poet; a Symbolist and Surrealist, his writings include "Sylvie" and *Les Chimères*; he became a famous for walking his pet lobster on a leash through the streets of Paris.

Mary Cassatt May 22, 1845; Artist; one of the most prominent American Impressionists, she also helped the Metropolitan Museum to amass its collection of French Impressionists through her friendships with the artists.

Sir Arthur Conan Doyle May 22, 1859; Writer; he created Sherlock Holmes, who was first introduced in *A Study in Scarlet*.

Willem Einthoven May 22, 1860; Dutch physiologist; for his work in developing the electro-cardiograph and its use in diagnosing various types of heart disease, he was awarded the Nobel Prize for medicine and physiology in 1924.

Marcel Breuer May 22, 1902; Architect, designer; he designed the Whitney Museum and the popular chair that bears his name.

Al Simmons May 22, 1903; Baseball player. Hall of Famer, 1953.

Harry Ritz May 22, 1906; Comedian, the youngest of the Ritz Brothers comedy team.

Sir Laurence Olivier May 22, 1907; Actor, producer, director; among his many and varied roles he won Oscars for his performances in Shakespeare's *Hamlet* and *Henry V*; he is considered the greatest stage actor of his generation.

Horton Smith May 22, 1908; Golfer; Masters winner, president of the PGA.

Vance Packard May 22, 1914; Noted author, journalist.

George Baker May 22, 1915; Cartoonist; an animator for Walt Disney, 1937–41, he created "The Sad Sack," one of the most popular comic strips of its day, while in the army during World War II.

Arnold Lobel May 22, 1923; Writer, illustrator; a winner of the Caldecott Medal, his many popular books for children include *Frog and Toad*.

Charles Aznavour May 22, 1924; French singer; most popular in the 1950s, he appeared in the film *Shoot the Piano Player*.

Quinn Martin May 22, 1927; TV producer; known for "The Fugitive," "Cannon," and "Streets of San Francisco."

Michael Constantine May 22, 1927; Actor; he won an Emmy for "Room 222."

T. Boone Pickens May 22, 1928; Entrepreneur; founder of Mesa Petroleum Company.

Marisol May 22, 1930; Venezuelan pop-art sculptor; known for large sculptures done in wood.

Peter Nero May 22, 1934; Pianist.

Garry Wills May 22, 1934; Author, journalist.

Frank Converse May 22, 1938; Actor; he appeared as Johnny Corso on the popular television series "NYPD."

Susan Strasberg May 22, 1938; Actress; she has appeared in numerous motion pictures since making her debut in *Picnic*.

Richard Benjamin May 22, 1938; Actor; one of his best known movies is *Goodbye Columbus*, 1969.

Michael Sarrazin May 22, 1940; Actor; his motion pictures include *The Flim Flam Man*, *They Shoot Horses Don't They?* and *The Reincarnation of Peter Proud*.

Paul Winfield May 22, 1941; Actor; a leading man, he has appeared on television and in motion pictures, including *Sounder*, *Damnation Alley* and *Star Trek II*.

Barbara Parkins May 22, 1942; Actress; she appeared in the motion picture *Valley of the Dolls* and the television series "Peyton Place."

Tommy John May 22, 1943; Baseball pitcher; he won 20 games in 1977.

Bernie Taupin May 22, 1950; English songwriter; he has written or co-written most of Elton John's gold record songs.

Rich Preston May 22, 1952; Canadian hockey player.

What's in a Number

Numerology is a study of numbers that some believe reveals character and personality. According to numerology, analyzing the numbers connected with your birthday can provide positive guidelines for your future.

The mystical properties of numbers have fascinated humans since long before the time of Pythagoras, the Greek philosopher and mathematician who lived in the sixth century B.C.E. and who is credited as one of the founders of the numbers system.

Famous people throughout history, including Julius Caesar, have "listened to the numbers." Even precivilization cave clans gave meaning to numerical symbols. Later, the Chinese, Hindus, Egyptians, Hebrews, Phoenicians, and Greeks similarly assigned cause and effect to them.

Numerologists can find striking similarities among those who share the same birthday. For example, George Washington, Senator Edward Kennedy, Boy Scout founder Robert Baden-Powell, United State Supreme Court Justice Charles Evans Whittaker, and two Nobel Prize winners were all born February 22. Numerology suggests that those born on this day can take charge of their own destiny, have the ability to touch greatness, and leave behind them lasting accomplishments.

As you read the numerological analysis for your birthday, think about the notable people who share it. Even if you don't take it seriously, you may be astonished at how many similarities you find in their lives and yours.

The following pages will tell you what qualities are associated with your first initial and what the numbers have to say about you based on your birthday.

Perhaps you'll get some good advice — after all, even a fortune cookie is right sometimes!

Find the First Letter of Your First Name and See What Numerology Says About You

A   Sensitive, individualistic.

B   Responsible, loyal.

C   Practical, restless.

D   Affectionate, creative.

E   Financially wise, responsible.

F   Introspective, inventive.

G   Fun-loving, an original thinker.

H   Selfless, restless, ingenious.

I   Original, artistic, congenial.

J   Dedicated, good-natured, thrifty.

K   Creative, steady, respected.

L   Cheerful, generous, active.

M   Steadfast, caring, wise.

N   Happy-go-lucky, courteous, brave.

O   Unselfish, outgoing, friendly.

P   Stimulating, admired, cerebral.

Q   Imaginative, carefree, sociable.

R   Warm-hearted, resourceful, kind.

S   Courageous, respected, able.

T   Thoughtful, economical, generous.

U   Pleasant, sophisticated, steady.

V   Progressive, charitable, gifted.

W   Level-headed, talented, friendly.

X   Likable, high spirited, smart.

Y   Lucky, upstanding, trustworthy.

Z   Discriminating, prudent, shrewd.

May 22:
What the Numbers
Say About You

You will work hard to build a better mouse trap; you are a born problem-solver. Unlike most people, you are given the option to labor for the benefit of a very broad section of humanity. You will inspire new traditions for future generations.

As a child your high energy is not as much of an asset as it becomes later in life. Children do not have the opportunity to be productive and see the results of their labors the way adults do. Parents, especially your father, are a positive influence on your creativity and ability for independent action.

You expand your interests early in life and grow far from your origins. After twenty-eight, you find it easier to employ your dynamic intuition and determination. When others fail to use their common sense, you "know" the right questions to ask to get answers that provide solutions. Your greatest successes may come through real estate or public service as your life unfolds.

Mid-life demands that you take control and focus your energy in order to see the results of your personal goals. It is in your best interest to be down to earth, empathetic and extremely honest in your business activities. Your destiny demands that intimate relationships and desires be your second priority.

Any overindulgence will be a distraction and could be destructive. If your instinct tells you that you are in over your head, call upon professionals for advice. Gather details; never gamble and draw your own conclusions.

Look forward to change. Accomplishments are important to you. You are a severe critic and a teacher throughout your life.

May Milestones in Sports and the Arts

1823

"Be it ever so humble..." John Howard Payne's "Home Sweet Home," the most popular song yet written by an American, premieres at Covent Garden in London.

1875

Thoroughbred *Aristides* wins the first Kentucky Derby at Churchill Downs, earning $2,850 in prize money.

1888

Popular actor DeWolf Hopper performs Ernest Thayer's "Casey at the Bat" at Wallach's Theater in New York City. It is the poem's first public recitation.

1904

Cy Young, of the Boston Americans baseball team, becomes the first major league pitcher to throw a perfect game (no opposing player reaches first base).

1893

The first motion picture exhibition using Thomas Edison's new kinetograph takes place at the Brooklyn Institute in New York. What's playing? A film of blacksmiths at work.

1900

Seventy-year-old Sir Eyre Massey Shaw of Great Britain proves that you're as young as you feel: he wins the 2–3-ton class yacht race to become the oldest gold medalist in Olympic history.

1911

Roy Harroun wins the first Indianapolis 500 auto race by averaging a blistering 74.5 mph.

1915

Babe Ruth, pitching for the Boston Red Sox, smashes his first major league home run off Yankee Jack Warhop at the Polo Grounds in New York.

1916

The Chicago Herald recognizes a dramatic new force in music when it becomes the first newspaper to use the word "jazz" in print.

1929

On With the Show, the first talking motion picture entirely in color, debuts at the Winter Garden in New York City.

1929

A mere 200 film industry insiders convene at the Hollywood Roosevelt Hotel for the first Academy Awards ceremony. *Wings* wins the golden statuette, not yet named Oscar, for Best Picture of 1928.

1933

Audiences ask "Who's Afraid of the Big Bad Wolf?" when Walt Disney's animated feature film *Three Little Pigs* premieres.

1936

Mutiny on the Bounty, starring Charles Laughton as Captain Bligh, wins the Academy Award for Best Picture of 1935.

1936

Reports of jockey Ralph Neves' death are greatly exaggerated. Pronounced dead after a fall at Bay Meadows Racetrack, Neves revives on the examining table and rushes back to the track to finish his race. He's confronted by the tumultuous cheers of astounded fans.

1936

Joe DiMaggio of the New York Yankees makes his major league debut against the St. Louis Browns. "Joltin' Joe" gets three hits to lead New York to a 14–5 win over the Browns.

1937

"The Edgar Bergen and Charlie McCarthy Show" premieres on NBC, to become one of the decade's top programs. Edgar Bergen is no dummy — and neither is his wooden sidekick Charlie McCarthy. The question is why a ventriloquist act should succeed on radio.

1937

Atlanta burns — with pride, this time — when Margaret Mitchell's *Gone With The Wind* wins the Pulitzer Prize for fiction.

1942

Bing Crosby cheers American GI's far from home when he records "White Christmas" for them this month. It will go on to become the best selling song in the U.S.

1944

"Oh, What a Beautiful Morning" for Richard Rogers and Oscar Hammerstein when *Oklahoma!* receives the Pulitzer Prize for theater.

1950

Gwendolyn Brooks becomes the first black woman to win the Pulitzer Prize for poetry with a collection titled *Annie Allen*.

1953

Sir Edmund Hillary of New Zealand and Nepalese Sherpa tribesman Tenzing Norkay are the first to reach the summit of Mt. Everest, tallest peak on earth. Why? Because it was there.

1954

The ultimate barrier in track — the four-minute mile — falls to Dr. Roger Bannister, who earns the title of "Fastest Man on Earth" with a mile clocked at 3 minutes, 59.4 seconds.

1959

Sam Snead becomes the first golfer to break 60 for 18 holes in a major tournament. He scores a 59, 11 strokes under par. To make things even better, he makes the record books while playing the Sam Snead Gold Festival in White Sulfur Springs, West Virginia.

1959

The first Grammy Awards go to Henry Mancini for Best Album (*The Music from Peter Gunn*), Ella Fitzgerald for Best Female Vocalist (*The Irving Berlin Songbook*), and Perry Como for Best Male Vocalist ("Catch a Falling Star").

1964

America dreams of surfin', cruisin', and dancin' in the California sun as The Beach Boys release their top single, "I Get Around."

1964

"The Dick Van Dyke Show" sweeps the Emmy Awards. It's named best comedy, and co-stars Dick Van Dyke and Mary Tyler Moore are voted best actor and actress.

1965

Cassius Clay, the future Muhammad Ali, "dances like a butterfly and stings like a bee" defending his heavyweight boxing title by knocking out Sonny Liston in the first round of a bout in Lewiston, Maine.

1968

It's spy versus spy at the Emmy Awards when "Mission: Impossible" wins for best dramatic series and its leading lady, Barbara Bain, for best actress. Bill Cosby is best actor for "I Spy."

1970

Good things come to those who wait. The Boston Bruins sweep the St. Louis Blues in four straight games to take hockey's Stanley Cup for the first time in 29 years.

1971

Three Dog Night brings "Joy to the World" when their single of that title tops *Billboard Magazine's* "Hot 100 List" for the entire month.

1972

"The Tonight Show Starring Johnny Carson" moves from New York City to "beautiful downtown Burbank."

1965

The Rolling Stones release their smash hit "I Can't Get No Satisfaction" this month.

1973

Secretariat wins the Kentucky Derby with a time of 1 minute, 59.4 seconds, a new track record.

1975

A Chorus Line, by Marvin Hamlisch and James Kirkwood, opens at the New York Shakespeare Festival's Newman Theater. It will go on to become the longest running musical ever to play on Broadway.

1976

Leonard Bernstein, Mstislav Rostropovich, Yehudi Menuhin, Isaac Stern, and Vladimir Horowitz are only a few of the luminaries who grace the "Concert of the Century" at Carnegie Hall, designed to benefit a $6.5 million fund drive to aid the concert hall.

1976

Dance superstars Mikhail Baryshnikov and Judith Jamison perform multiple *pas de deux* in *Pas de Duke*, Alvin Ailey's homage to jazz great Duke Ellington.

1977

The studio is nervous and the critics skeptical when a little known filmmaker releases a *big*-budget sci-fi movie about an empire in space. But "the Force" is with George Lucas as *Star Wars* becomes one of the top five grossing films of all time.

1977

It's a bird, it's a plane... no, it's daredevil toy designer George Willig, scaling one of the towers of the World Trade Center, New York's tallest building. Amused, police fine Willig $1.10 or 1 cent for every story climbed.

1979

Four and a half days of tennis, anyone? Amateur tennis players Jeff Sutton and Ricky Tolston play a match in Kingston, North Carolina that lasts 105 hours, the longest ever.

1980

Larry Bird of the Boston Celtics is named NBA Rookie of the Year.

1980

Maxie Anderson and his son, Kris, complete the first nonstop, transcontinental balloon flight aboard the *Kitty Hawk*. The daring aeronauts cover some 3,100 miles from California to Quebec in 4 days.

1983

Michael Jackson's single "Beat It" goes gold this month.

1984

Julio Iglesias' and Willie Nelson's sentimental duet, "To All the Girls I've Loved Before," goes gold this month.

1987

Beverly Hills Cop II, starring Eddie Murphy, grosses over $26,300,000 over the Memorial Day weekend to set a new 3-day record.

1987

Mario Andretti drives his new Lola automobile around the 2 and 1/2 mile oval at 218.204 mph to set a record for the fastest lap in the history of the Indianapolis Motor Speedway.

1987

Sugar Town Dandy, a frog among frogs, leaps 19 feet, 7 1/4 inches to win the annual Calaveras County Jumping Frog Jubilee. The $500 in prize money, awarded to commemorate Mark Twain's famous story, ought to buy a deluxe lily pad.

1987

August Wilson's *Fences* wins the New York Drama Critics Circle Award for best new play of the 1986–1987 season. *Les Misèrables* is chosen best musical.

1989

Platinum blonde Madonna's *Like a Prayer* album goes double platinum this month.

Thought Provokers

■ Babe Ruth was 32 years old when he hit his record 60 home runs in 1927. He was 40 when he hit his last one on May 25, 1935.

■ Zeuxis and Parrhasius, who lived in Greece about 400 B.C., were rival artists who accepted a challenge to test their skills. On the appointed day, Zeuxis produced a painting of a bunch of grapes so realistic that birds came to peck at them. He then bid Parrhasius to remove the curtain from *his* painting, only to be told by his rival, "The curtain *is* the picture." Zeuxis conceded defeat, admitting that his grapes had fooled only the birds, but Parrhasius's curtain had fooled him!

■ The first confirmed kite flying occurred in China in about 400 B.C. Kites were first seen in Europe in 1589.

■ An unfinished pyramid, on top of which rests an eye within a triangle, appears on the back of every U.S. one dollar bill. It is part of the reverse side of the Great Seal of the United States and symbolizes the strength and growth of the Union.

◼ Leonardo da Vinci was 51 when he painted the *Mona Lisa*.

◼ The Achilles tendon, which joins the calf muscles of the leg to the heel bone, can resist a tension of 1,000 pounds.

◼ One of history's greatest libraries flourished in Alexandria, Egypt more than 2,000 years ago. It contained over 500,000 volumes of the works of such great scholars as Aristophanes, who edited the works of Homer. By 91 A.D., it had been utterly destroyed by war and fire, leaving neither a trace of the structure nor a shred of the works it contained.

◼ The King James Version of the Bible contains 774,746 words and 3,566,480 letters.

◼ Ferdinand Magellan began the epic voyage that would prove the earth round at age 39. When he was killed in the Philippines, Juan Sebastian del Cano took command and completed the expedition at 46. Of the five vessels that began the voyage, only the *Vittoria* survived, thus becoming the first ship to sail completely around the earth.

◼ At 32 Joseph Story of Massachusetts was the youngest person ever to become a member of the United States Supreme Court. At 33 William Johnston of North Carolina was a close second. Harlan Stone of New York was the oldest, joining that august body at 69. James Iredell of North Carolina left the court at the youngest age, 48. The oldest person ever to serve was "The Great Dissenter,"

Oliver Wendell Holmes, Jr., also of Massachusetts, who left the Court at 91. William O. Douglas of Connecticut served the longest, 36 years.

■ Tutankhamen, ("King Tut"), the pharaoh who ruled all of ancient Egypt nearly 3,500 years ago, and whose undisturbed tomb yielded fabulous treasures, was 18 when he died.

■ In 1853, an army of 500,000 composed entirely of women and led by female officers was formed in Nanking, China during a rebellion.

■ One in 344 Americans is a postal employee. Their total exceeds the population of each of six states and that of Washington, D.C.

■ Christopher Columbus went to sea at age 14. He made his epic voyage to discover American when he was 41.

■ At the rate of a million dollars a minute, it would require more than 437 years to spend an amount equal the national debt. Even at one million dollars *per second* it would take well over seven years.

■ In China, canals and rivers were controlled by a series of gates in the 3rd century B.C.

■ Alfred Einstein emerged as one of the greatest scientists in history when he published his theory of relativity at age 26. In his last public utterance 50 years later, he appealed for an end to the nuclear arms race, a consequence of his great discovery.

■ The story of George Washington's false teeth is familiar to many, although it is now believed they were not made of wood. Artificial teeth are mentioned in a 1609 play by the noted English playwright Ben Jonson. And Martial, a Roman poet who lived in the first century, referred to them in one of his works: "You use, without a blush, *false teeth* and hair: But, Laelia, your squint is past repair."

■ Michelangelo began his earliest surviving sculpture, *Madonna of the Stairs*, when he was 15 years old. He became the foremost sculptor of his age when he finished his *Pieta* at 24. When only 26, he began his great *David*, carved from an unwanted block of marble he found that had been lying 46 years in a courtyard of the Cathedral of Florence. He was working on his final sculpture, the *Rondanini Pieta*, within a week of his death at 89.

■ The Chinese began deep drilling for water and natural gas in the 1st century. Europeans did not accomplish this until 1126, eleven centuries later.

■ In early times, heavy penalties were imposed on bakers for selling short weights or measures. To avoid the risk of fines, they began adding an extra loaf to each dozen, whence comes the term "baker's dozen."

■ Wolfgang Amadeus Mozart began playing the harpsichord at 3, composed simple pieces at 5, and performed in Vienna for the Holy Roman Emperor at 6. By 8 he had performed for the kings of France and England. He wrote his first opera at age 12. At his death at 32, he had composed over 600 works in virtually every form.

At Your Age...

We routinely spend many hours in such activities as dressing, bathing, eating, walking, traveling, reading, studying, working, and entertaining ourselves. Have you ever thought about the time you spend daily, weekly, monthly, or even over a year doing these things? Most of us do not realize how those hours mount up to a sizeable portion of our total lives. You might be surprised.

Throughout our lives, our bodies are also a constant beehive of activity. They do most important things without our even being consciously aware of them. Most of these activities protect vital functions, keep us healthy, and even keep us alive. Our hearts beat, we sleep, grow new body cells and hair, cough, sneeze, bat our eyes, breathe, and many other things.

The cumulative statistics on some of our most vital activities are startling. They will of course vary for individuals. You've been busy, as you will see by the following chart.

AT YOUR AGE

At This Age	You Have Blinked This Many Times	You Have Breathed This Many Times	You Have Eaten This Many Meals	Your Heart Has Beaten This Many Times	It Has Pumped This Many Gallons of Blood	You Have Slept This Many Hours	You Have Slept This Many Days
1	2,371,770	6,016,982	1,569	69,251,400	1,352,566	6,022	250
2	6,166,602	12,033,964	2,883	127,107,000	2,482,558	10,402	433
3	10,593,906	18,050,947	4,069	184,962,600	3,612,550	14,052	585
4	15,160,180	24,080,284	5,204	237,558,600	4,639,816	17,566	731
5	19,840,473	30,097,267	6,299	290,154,600	5,667,082	20,924	871
6	24,615,636	36,114,249	7,394	337,491,000	6,591,621	24,172	1,007
7	29,438,235	42,131,232	8,489	384,827,400	7,516,160	27,366	1,140
8	34,353,323	48,160,569	9,587	432,163,800	8,440,699	30,477	1,269
9	39,375,150	54,177,552	10,682	479,500,200	9,365,238	33,441	1,393
10	44,400,140	60,194,534	11,777	526,836,600	10,289,777	36,401	1,516
11	49,425,130	66,211,516	12,872	574,173,000	11,214,316	39,361	1,640
12	54,463,888	72,240,854	13,970	621,509,400	12,138,855	42,329	1,763
13	59,488,878	78,257,836	15,065	668,845,800	13,063,394	45,289	1,887
14	64,513,868	84,274,819	16,160	716,182,200	13,987,933	48,250	2,010
15	69,538,858	90,291,801	17,255	763,518,600	14,912,472	51,210	2,133
16	74,577,615	96,321,139	18,353	805,595,400	15,734,285	54,178	2,257
17	79,602,605	102,338,121	19,448	847,672,200	16,556,097	57,138	2,380
18	84,627,595	108,355,104	20,543	889,749,000	17,377,910	60,098	2,504
19	89,652,585	114,372,086	21,638	929,196,000	18,148,359	63,059	2,627
20	94,691,342	120,401,424	22,736	968,643,000	18,918,808	66,027	2,751

AT YOUR AGE

At This Age	You Have Blinked This Many Times	You Have Breathed This Many Times	You Have Eaten This Many Meals	Your Heart Has Beaten This Many Times	It Has Pumped This Many Gallons of Blood	You Have Slept This Many Hours	You Have Slept This Many Days
21	99,716,332	126,418,406	23,831	1,008,090,000	19,689,257	68,987	2,874
22	104,741,322	132,435,388	24,926	1,047,537,000	20,459,707	71,947	2,997
23	109,766,312	138,452,371	26,021	1,086,984,000	21,230,156	74,907	3,121
24	114,805,069	144,481,708	27,119	1,126,431,000	22,000,605	77,875	3,244
25	119,830,059	150,498,691	28,214	1,165,878,000	22,771,054	80,835	3,368
26	124,855,049	156,515,673	29,309	1,205,325,000	23,541,503	83,796	3,491
27	129,880,039	162,532,656	30,404	1,244,772,000	24,311,953	86,756	3,614
28	134,918,797	168,561,993	31,502	1,284,219,000	25,082,402	89,724	3,738
29	139,943,787	174,578,976	32,597	1,323,666,000	25,852,851	92,684	3,861
30	144,968,777	180,595,958	33,692	1,363,113,000	26,623,300	95,644	3,985
31	149,993,767	186,612,940	34,787	1,402,560,000	27,393,750	98,605	4,108
32	155,032,524	192,642,278	35,885	1,442,007,000	28,164,199	101,573	4,232
33	160,057,514	198,659,260	36,980	1,481,454,000	28,934,648	104,533	4,355
34	165,082,504	204,676,243	38,075	1,520,901,000	29,705,097	107,493	4,478
35	170,107,494	210,693,225	39,170	1,560,348,000	30,475,546	110,453	4,602
36	175,146,251	216,722,563	40,268	1,599,795,000	31,245,996	113,421	4,725
37	180,171,241	222,739,545	41,363	1,639,242,000	32,016,445	116,382	4,849
38	185,196,231	228,756,528	42,458	1,678,689,000	32,786,894	119,342	4,972
39	190,221,221	234,773,510	43,553	1,718,136,000	33,557,343	122,302	5,095
40	195,259,978	240,802,848	44,651	1,757,583,000	34,327,792	125,270	5,219

AT YOUR AGE

At This Age	You Have Blinked This Many Times	You Have Breathed This Many Times	You Have Eaten This Many Meals	Your Heart Has Beaten This Many Times	It Has Pumped This Many Gallons of Blood	You Have Slept This Many Hours	You Have Slept This Many Days
41	200,284,968	246,819,830	45,746	1,797,030,000	35,098,242	128,230	5,343
42	205,309,958	252,836,812	46,841	1836,477,000	35,868,691	131,190	5,466
43	210,334,948	258,853,795	47,936	1,875,924,000	36,639,140	134,151	5,589
44	215,373,706	264,883,132	49,034	1,915,371,000	37,409,589	137,119	5,713
45	220,398,696	270,900,115	50,129	1,954,818,000	38,180,039	140,079	5,836
46	225,423,686	276,917,097	51,224	1,992,687,120	38,919,670	143,039	5,959
47	230,448,676	282,934,080	52,319	2,030,556,240	39,659,301	145,999	6,083
48	235,487,433	288,963,417	53,417	2,068,425,360	40,398,932	148,968	6,207
49	240,512,423	294,980,400	54,512	2,106,294,480	41,138,564	151,928	6,330
50	245,537,413	300,997,382	55,607	2,144,163,600	41,878,195	154,888	6,453
51	250,562,403	307,014,364	56,702	2,182,032,720	42,617,826	157,848	6,577
52	255,601,160	313,043,702	57,800	2,219,901,840	43,357,457	160,816	6,700
53	260,626,150	319,060,684	58,895	2,257,770,960	44,097,089	163,776	6,824
54	265,651,140	325,077,667	59,990	2,295,640,080	44,836,720	166,737	6,947
55	270,676,130	331,094,649	61,085	2,333,509,200	45,576,351	169,697	7,070
56	275,714,887	337,123,987	62,183	2,371,378,320	46,315,982	172,665	7,194
57	280,739,877	343,140,969	63,278	2,409,247,440	47,055,614	175,625	7,317
58	285,764,867	349,157,952	64,373	2,447,116,560	47,795,245	178,585	7,441
59	290,789,857	355,174,934	65,468	2,484,985,680	48,534,876	181,545	7,564
60	295,831,786	361,204,272	66,566	2,522,854,800	49,274,507	184,511	7,688

AT YOUR AGE

At This Age	You Have Blinked This Many Times	You Have Breathed This Many Times	You Have Eaten This Many Meals	Your Heart Has Beaten This Many Times	It Has Pumped This Many Gallons of Blood	You Have Slept This Many Hours	You Have Slept This Many Days
61	300,882,992	367,221,254	67,661	2,559,672,000	49,993,593	187,440	7,810
62	305,957,044	373,238,236	68,756	2,596,489,200	50,712,679	190,343	7,930
63	311,053,736	379,255,219	69,851	2,633,306,400	51,431,765	193,221	8,050
64	316,186,891	385,284,556	70,949	2,670,123,600	52,150,851	196,080	8,170
65	321,328,255	391,301,539	72,044	2,706,940,800	52,869,937	198,906	8,287
66	326,491,654	397,318,521	73,139	2,742,706,080	53,568,478	201,706	8,404
67	331,676,889	403,335,504	74,234	2,778,471,360	54,267,018	204,482	8,520
68	336,898,030	409,364,841	75,332	2,814,236,640	54,965,559	207,239	8,634
69	342,126,350	415,381,824	76,427	2,850,001,920	55,664,100	209,965	8,748
70	347,375,922	421,398,806	77,522	2,885,767,200	56,362,640	212,666	8,861
71	352,646,555	427,415,788	78,617	2,921,532,480	57,061,181	215,342	8,972
72	357,952,557	433,445,126	79,715	2,957,297,760	57,759,721	218,002	9,083
73	363,264,745	439,462,108	80,810	2,993,063,040	58,458,262	220,631	9,192
74	368,597,430	445,479,091	81,905	3,028,828,320	59,156,803	223,236	9,301
75	373,950,428	451,496,073	83,000	3,064,593,600	59,855,343	225,817	9,409
76	379,338,277	457,525,411	84,098	3,098,781,000	60,523,066	228,383	9,515
77	384,731,354	463,542,393	85,193	3,132,968,400	61,190,789	230,918	9,621
78	390,144,200	469,559,376	86,288	3,167,155,800	61,858,511	233,431	9,726
79	395,576,637	475,576,358	87,383	3,201,343,200	62,526,234	235,920	9,830
80	401,043,426	481,605,696	88,481	3,235,530,600	63,193,957	238,395	9,933

AT YOUR AGE

At This Age	You Have Blinked This Many Times	You Have Breathed This Many Times	You Have Eaten This Many Meals	Your Heart Has Beaten This Many Times	It Has Pumped This Many Gallons of Blood	You Have Slept This Many Hours	You Have Slept This Many Days
81	406,514,519	487,622,678	89,576	3,269,718,000	63,861,679	240,840	10,035
82	412,004,679	493,639,660	90,671	3,303,905,400	64,529,402	243,263	10,135
83	417,513,734	499,656,643	91,766	3,338,092,800	65,197,125	245,665	10,236
84	423,056,660	505,685,980	92,864	3,372,280,200	65,864,847	248,051	10,335
85	428,602,998	511,702,963	93,959	3,406,467,600	66,532,570	250,409	10,433
86	434,167,726	517,719,945	95,054	3,438,025,200	67,148,929	252,747	10,531
87	439,750,678	523,736,928	96,149	3,469,582,800	67,765,289	255,063	10,627
88	445,367,036	529,766,265	97,247	3,501,140,400	68,381,648	257,364	10,723
89	450,985,946	535,783,248	98,342	3,532,698,000	68,998,007	259,639	10,818
90	456,622,593	541,800,230	99,437	3,564,255,600	69,614,367	261,893	10,912
91	462,276,818	547,817,212	100,532	3,595,813,200	70,230,726	264,127	11,005
92	467,964,000	553,846,550	101,630	3,627,370,800	70,847,085	266,347	11,097
93	473,652,906	559,863,532	102,725	3,658,928,400	71,463,445	268,541	11,189
94	479,358,918	565,880,515	103,820	3,690,486,000	72,079,804	270,715	11,279
95	485,081,883	571,897,497	104,915	3,722,043,600	72,696,164	272,869	11,369
96	490,837,374	577,926,835	106,013	3,753,601,200	73,312,523	275,010	11,458
97	496,593,789	583,943,817	107,108	3,785,158,800	73,928,882	277,126	11,546
98	502,366,703	589,960,799	108,203	3,816,716,400	74,545,242	279,223	11,634
99	508,155,967	595,977,782	109,298	3,848,274,000	75,161,601	281,301	11,720
100	513,977,341	602,007,119	110,396	3,879,831,600	75,777,960	283,366	11,806